THE BEST 50

QUICHES

the editorial staff of Bristol Publishing Enterprises

BRISTOL PUBLISHING ENTERPRISES
San Leandro, California

Printed in the United States of America.

ISBN 1-55867-203-6

Cover design: Frank J. Paredes
Cover photography: John A. Benson
Food stylist: Susan Massey

ABOUT QUICHE

There have been many delightful modern changes to the original Quiche à la Lorraine recipe, a pastry tart filled with custard and bacon or ham. When you think of quiche, you might assume that it contains cheese, but it is optional and is not "correct" as far as the traditional tart. Fortunately, today's cook is not so concerned about being "correct," and any pie shell filled with any savory mixture — cheese, vegetables, seafood or meats — and custard is referred to as a quiche.

This special custard-filled tart is said to originate in France, but as it is from the region of Alsace, bordering on Germany, it may be of German origin, as the borders have changed often through history. Indeed, the name may be a transition from *kuche*, the German word for *kitchen*.

The quiche is a most versatile dish. It is at home almost every-where, in a wide variety of containers, and on every occasion. It can be a delicious appetizer, a luncheon or supper entrée or a side dish, and it's perfect for the brunch or buffet table. It can be filled with just

about anything, which makes it an excellent way to use small amounts of leftovers. And it's a boon to the host or hostess, because its components can be prepared ahead of time, and the filled shell covered with custard and popped into the oven at the last minute.

EQUIPMENT

The original quiche was probably baked in a pottery plate, but there are many other ways to go about it. Obviously, the larger the pan or dish, the thinner the quiche will be, and the shorter the required baking time. Here are some other possible containers:

- a flan ring with a removable bottom
- a porcelain quiche dish
- an ordinary pie plate
- a layer cake pan
- muffin cups of any size

- individual tart pans
- an 8- or 9-inch square baking pan

SERVINGS

- An 8- or 9-inch quiche will serve 4 to 6 people as an entrée.
- A 10-inch quiche will serve 6 to 8 people as an entrée.
- Cut the quiche into 12 to 16 small wedges for appetizer servings.

CREATE YOUR OWN QUICHE RECIPE

It's easy to create your own 9-inch quiche recipe using the following formula (a 10-inch shell will hold $1\frac{1}{2}$ times as much):

- 2 eggs or $\frac{1}{2}$ cup egg substitute

- 1 cup cream, milk or evaporated milk (milk can be low-fat)
- 1-2 cups vegetable, meat or cheese filling, or a combination
- herbs or spices of choice
- 1 prepared quiche shell

ABOUT QUICHE

ABOUT QUICHE SHELLS

Pastry crusts get their flakiness from butter or other fats. The larger the pieces of fat that remain in the dough after it is rolled, the flakier the crust will be. It is important to work the dough as fast and as little as possible, and to make sure the ingredients are very cold. You can also chill the dough before it is rolled.

The more fat the dough contains, the faster and darker it will brown. Expect doughs containing fat — egg yolks, milk and butter — to develop a deeper golden color than nonpastry doughs, such as French bread dough and pizza dough.

If you make the dough with a food processor, work very fast so the dough will not become overworked and warm. Place dry ingredients in the workbowl. Add cold butter or shortening and pulse briefly until mixture resembles coarse crumbs. Add cold milk or water a little at a time, and pulse for 1 to 2 seconds, until the mixture resembles cottage cheese. You may not need all of the liquid. Gather dough into a ball with your hands. Chill it for about 30 minutes before rolling.

CLASSIC PASTRY QUICHE SHELL

The less milk you use, and the less you handle the dough, the flakier this pastry will be.

1 cup plus 2 tbs. flour
pinch salt
3 tbs. cold butter
3 tbs. vegetable shortening
2-5 tbs. very cold milk

Heat oven to 450°. Place flour and salt in a bowl. With 2 knives or a pastry blender, cut butter and shortening into flour until mixture is fine and mealy. Add cold milk 1 tablespoon at a time and mix dough gently until it just gathers into a firm, crumbly ball. Do not exert pressure to force dough together. Roll between 2 sheets of waxed paper or on a lightly floured surface. Line pan, being careful not to stretch pastry. Prick all over surface, including sides, with the tines of a fork. Partially bake shell on lowest rack of oven for 8 to 10 minutes or until pastry is set; it may be lightly browned. Check after 5 minutes and gently push down puffy spots. Cool for at least 10 minutes before filling.

Makes one 9-inch quiche shell

CHEESE PASTRY QUICHE SHELL

Make this easily with a food processor. Pulse all ingredients, except egg yolks and milk, until crumbly. Add milk through the feed tube, a tablespoon at a time, and pulse briefly until the dough will come together when pressed with your fingers. It should not form a ball in the workbowl.

1½ cups flour
¼ cup grated Parmesan cheese
pinch salt
pinch cayenne pepper
pinch dry mustard
¼ cup cold butter
4 egg yolks, slightly beaten
1-3 tbs. very cold milk

Heat oven to 450°. Place flour, cheese, salt, cayenne and dry mustard in a bowl. With 2 knives or a pastry blender, cut butter into flour until mixture is fine and mealy. Make a well in the center. With a fork, work yolks into dry ingredients. Add only enough milk, 1 tablespoon at a time, to make dough gather. Shape into a smooth ball and roll out between 2 sheets of waxed peper or on a lightly floured surface. Line pan, being careful not to stretch pastry. Prick all over surface, including sides, with the tines of a fork. Partially bake shell on lowest rack of oven for 8 to 12 minutes or until lightly browned and set. Check after 5 minutes and gently push down puffy spots. Cool for at least 10 minutes before filling.

Makes one 9-inch quiche shell

FRENCH BREAD DOUGH QUICHE SHELL

The texture is a little different than a pastry dough, but this quiche shell has significantly less fat and fewer calories. If the edges brown too fast while the quiche is baking, cover them with strips of foil.

1 cup lukewarm water
1 tsp. salt
½ tbs. sugar
3½ cups bread flour
1 tsp. fast-acting yeast

Make dough in a bread machine: Place ingredients in the bread pan in the order given, or according to manufacturer's instructions (a few bread machines specifically call for wet ingredients to be last). Set the machine on the dough cycle.

Make dough by hand: Dissolve yeast in water. Add sugar, salt and flour and knead into a stiff dough. Let rise in a warm, draft-free location until doubled in size. Punch down. Let rise until doubled in size.

On a lightly floured surface, roll out dough and fit into a quiche pan. Do not prebake before filling.

Makes one 9-inch quiche shell

PUFF PASTRY QUICHE SHELL

Frozen puff pastry makes a flavorful crust with little work. Thaw only one sheet from the package, and leave the other sheet in the freezer for another use.

1 sheet frozen puff pastry, thawed at
room temperature for 30 minutes

Spray a 9-inch square or round baking pan with nonstick cooking spray. The pastry comes in square sheets. Leave square for a 9-inch square baking pan. If using a round pan, gather dough into a disk before rolling it into a circle. Roll dough on a lightly floured work surface and fit into pan. Prick bottom and sides well with the tines of a fork. Do not prebake before filling.

Makes one 9-inch quiche shell

PURCHASED PIZZA DOUGH OR
FRENCH BREAD DOUGH QUICHE SHELL

Look in your grocer's refrigerator case for tubes of ready-made pizza dough, French bread dough and breadstick dough. Rolled to fit your pan, they make wonderful, easy-to-use quiche crusts, and they're low in fat.

1 tube ready-to-use pizza dough,
French bread dough or breadstick dough

On a lightly floured surface, roll dough into a circle. Fit dough into a quiche pan. If using breadstick dough, twist lengths together, form a ball and then roll out dough. Do not prebake before filling.

Makes one 9-inch quiche shell

EGG ROLL WRAPPER QUICHE SHELLS

Egg roll wrappers and won ton wrappers make shells for individual quiches and appetizer-sized quiches in a flash. Use egg roll wrappers in regular-sized muffin cups. Won ton wrappers can be used in miniature muffin cups for one-bite servings for party food. These wrappers are usually found in refrigerator cases in the produce section of the supermarket.

1 pkg. egg roll wrappers or won ton wrappers

Heat oven to 325°. Lightly grease muffin cups, or spray with nonstick cooking spray. Line each cup with a wrapper. Trim excess dough if desired, or flare out the edges in a decorative manner. Fill with desired custard and filling and bake according to size.

- Baking time for 3-inch cups is 10 to 15 minutes.
- Baking time for 1½-inch cups is 7 to 10 minutes.

Makes about seventy 1½-inch quiche shells or twenty 3-inch quiche shells

CRUSTLESS QUICHE

Crustless quiche makes a great addition to a brunch buffet. Make small versions in miniature muffin cups as finger food for a party. Choose any recipe for quiche and omit the prepared quiche shell. (Low-fat custard turns out a little watery without a crust for a base.) You can also make quiche squares — put your filling and custard into an 9-inch square pan that has been sprayed with nonstick cooking spray, and when it is done cut it into squares.

Preheat oven to 325°. Cut parchment paper to fit your pan, or spray a nonstick surface with nonstick cooking spray.

- Bake a 9-inch quiche for 25 to 30 minutes, until center is set and top is lightly browned.
- Bake miniature quiche bites (about 1½ inches) for 12 to 15 minutes.

CLASSIC CUSTARD

*To complement the filling you choose, you can add 2 to 4 tbs.
chopped fresh herbs, or 2 to 4 tsp. dried herbs.*

1 cup whipping cream, half-and-half or whole milk
2 eggs
1/2 tsp. salt
pinch cayenne pepper
freshly ground pepper, optional

Beat ingredients together until well blended.

RICH CUSTARD

This custard works well with shellfish quiche, such as crab, shrimp or lobster, or for any extra-special quiche.

1 cup whipping cream or half-and-half
1 egg
2 egg yolks
salt to taste
pinch cayenne pepper
freshly ground pepper, optional

Beat ingredients together until well blended.

SOUR CREAM CUSTARD

For a rich-tasting quiche, use this custard. It goes well with subtly flavored ingredients, such as mushrooms and spinach, as well as strongly flavored ingredients, such as smoked fish and meats.

1 cup sour cream
2 eggs
salt and freshly ground pepper to taste
pinch cayenne pepper

Beat ingredients together until well blended.

LOW-FAT CUSTARD

*Egg substitute is a low-fat, low-cholesterol product that is 99%
egg whites. It can be used in the same way as beaten eggs;
1/4 cup egg substitute is equal to 1 large egg. Use it in any quiche
recipe in place of eggs, but choose a filling that is low in moisture. Tomatoes, mushrooms and other high-moisture vegetables
paired with this custard produce a somewhat watery result.*

1/2 cup egg substitute
1 cup evaporated skimmed milk
salt and freshly ground pepper to taste

Beat ingredients together until well blended.

QUICHE LORRAINE

*Created in the French region of Alsace-Lorraine, this
is the original quiche. You can use aged cheddar or munster
instead of Gruyère cheese, and Swiss cheese works well, too.*

6-8 slices bacon
8 oz. Gruyère cheese, grated
prepared quiche shell (see pages 5-15)
custard (see pages 16-19)

Heat oven to 375°. In a large skillet, fry bacon over medium-high heat until very crisp. Drain on paper towels and crumble. Sprinkle bacon and cheese into prepared quiche shell. Pour custard over bacon and cheese and bake for 35 to 45 minutes, or until custard is set and top is lightly browned. Rest quiche for 5 minutes before cutting.

Makes one 9-inch quiche

CLASSIC QUICHES

VARIATIONS

- **HAM AND CHEESE QUICHE:** Substitute ½ lb. ham, cut into ¼-inch cubes, for the bacon.

- **PANCETTA PARMESAN QUICHE:** Substitute ½ lb. sliced pancetta (Italian peppered bacon) for the bacon and 1 cup (4 oz.) freshly grated Parmesan cheese for the Gruyère.

CHEESE QUICHE

The simplest quiche to make is a cheese quiche. Use sharp cheddar, Gruyère, blue-veined or any other strongly flavored cheese for this quiche.

custard (see pages 16-19)
1½ cups grated or crumbled cheese
prepared quiche shell (see pages 5-15)

Heat oven to 375°. In a bowl, mix custard with cheese. Pour into a prepared quiche shell. Bake for 35 to 45 minutes, until custard is set and top is lightly browned. Rest quiche for 5 minutes before cutting.

Makes one 9-inch quiche

TOMATO QUICHE

This is a great way to show off home-grown tomatoes when they are overflowing in the garden. Use tomatoes that are just ripe. Overly ripe tomatoes make the mixture watery.

2 cups diced peeled, seeded tomatoes
1/4 cup chopped fresh flat-leaf parsley
prepared quiche shell (see pages 5-15)
custard (see pages 16-19)

Heat oven to 375°. Sprinkle diced tomatoes and parsley evenly in prepared quiche shell. Cover with custard. Bake for 40 to 45 minutes, or until custard is set and top is lightly browned. Rest quiche for 5 minutes before cutting.

Makes one 9-inch quiche

ARTICHOKE QUICHE

*You can use frozen artichoke hearts for this recipe, but
you must drain them very well after you cook them.*

12 small artichokes
2 tbs. white wine vinegar
1 tsp. salt
3-4 whole peppercorns
bay leaf
2-3 tbs. butter
1 small leek, cut in half lengthwise, thinly sliced
prepared quiche shell (see pages 5-15)
2 tbs. chopped fresh flat-leaf parsley
2 tbs. chopped fresh thyme, or 2 tsp. dried
custard (see pages 16-19)

Heat oven to 375°. Trim leaves from artichokes so that only the edible part of the heart remains. Cover with boiling water, add vinegar, salt, peppercorns and bay leaf, and cook for 10 minutes or until tender. Drain well. Shake in a pot over heat to remove excess moisture.

In a medium skillet, melt butter and sauté leek over medium heat until soft, about 5 minutes. Add artichokes and stir to coat. Cool slightly. Spread artichoke-leek mixture in quiche shell. Add herbs to custard and stir. Pour custard over artichoke mixture and bake for 35 to 45 minutes, or until custard is set and top is lightly browned. Rest quiche for 5 minutes before cutting.

Makes one 9-inch quiche

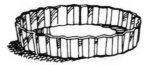

ASPARAGUS-PARMESAN QUICHE

You'll think of fresh asparagus with hollandaise sauce when you taste this quiche.

½ lb. fresh asparagus
1 cup freshly grated Parmesan cheese
prepared quiche shell (see pages 5-15)
¼ cup fresh lemon juice
½ tsp. grated fresh lemon peel (zest)
custard (see pages 16-19)

Heat oven to 375°. Cut tough ends from asparagus and discard. Cut asparagus into 1-inch pieces and steam or cook in boiling water until tender-crisp. Drain well and toss with Parmesan cheese until well coated. Cool slightly. Arrange in quiche shell. Add lemon juice and zest to custard, stir and pour custard over asparagus. Bake for 35 to 45 minutes, or until custard is set and top is lightly browned. Rest quiche for 5 minutes before cutting.

Makes one 9-inch quiche

LOW-FAT ASPARAGUS AND ROASTED RED PEPPER QUICHE

If you're watching fat, but love asparagus and quiche, try this delicious version. To make cutting the fat worthwhile, choose a bread quiche shell.

8 oz. asparagus, trimmed
1/2 large red onion, diced
1 cup egg substitute
1 cup evaporated skimmed milk
salt and freshly ground pepper to taste
1/2 cup freshly grated Parmesan cheese
1 cup diced roasted red bell pepper
prepared quiche shell (see pages 5-15)

Heat oven to 375°. Steam asparagus or cook in boiling water until tender-crisp; drain well and set aside. Spray a skillet with nonstick cooking spray. Sauté onion over medium heat until soft, about 3 to 5 minutes; set aside. In a large bowl, mix together egg substitute and skimmed milk. Stir in salt, pepper and Parmesan. Add asparagus, onion and diced pepper and stir to blend. Pour mixture into prepared quiche shell. Bake for 35 to 45 minutes, until center is set and top is lightly browned. Rest quiche for 5 minutes before cutting.

Makes one 9-inch quiche

GREEN BEAN AND ALMOND QUICHE

The familiar combination of green beans and almonds is delicious in a quiche.

½ lb. fresh green beans, trimmed
2 tbs. butter
2 oz. slivered almonds
3 large shallots, diced
prepared quiche shell (see pages 5-15)
custard (see pages 16-19)

Heat oven to 375°. Cut green beans diagonally into 1-inch pieces. Steam or cook in boiling water until tender-crisp; drain well and set aside. In a small skillet, melt butter, add almonds and sauté over medium-high heat until they begin to brown, about 2 to 3 minutes. Add beans and shallots and sauté for 2 to 3 minutes. Cool slightly. Distribute vegetables and almonds in prepared quiche shell and cover with custard. Bake for 35 to 45 minutes, or until custard is set and top is lightly browned. Rest quiche for 5 minutes before cutting.

Makes one 9-inch quiche

QUICHE NIÇOISE

You can also use kalamata olives or other imported cured black olives, but not California ripe olives.

½ lb. fresh green beans, trimmed, cut into ¼-inch pieces
custard (see pages 16-19)
2 medium plum tomatoes, peeled, seeded, diced
½ cup niçoise olives, well drained, cut into slivers
prepared quiche shell (see pages 5-15)

Heat oven to 375°. Steam beans or cook in boiling water until tender-crisp; drain well and cool slightly. Mix together custard, beans, tomatoes and olives. Pour mixture into prepared quiche shell. Bake for 40 to 45 minutes, until custard is set and top is lightly browned. Rest quiche for 5 minutes before cutting.

Makes one 9-inch quiche

SUNNY CARROT QUICHE

This sunny quiche is bright orange and yellow. Tarragon adds just the right touch of flavor.

3-4 carrots, peeled, cut into ¼-inch rounds
2-3 tbs. butter
3 large shallots, diced
prepared quiche shell (see pages 5-15)
¼ cup chopped fresh tarragon, or 1 heaping tbs. dried
custard (see pages 16-19)

Heat oven to 375°. Steam carrots or cook in boiling water until tender-crisp. In a medium skillet, melt butter and sauté shallots over medium heat for 2 to 3 minutes. Cool slightly. Add carrots and stir to coat completely. Arrange carrots and shallots in prepared quiche shell. Mix tarragon with custard and pour over carrot-shallot mixture. Bake for 35 to 45 minutes, or until custard is set and top is lightly browned. Rest quiche for 5 minutes before cutting.

Makes one 9-inch quiche

SWEET CORN AND PEPPER QUICHE

*Use red, green and yellow bell peppers, if you have them,
for a colorful quiche.*

2 cups corn kernels, fresh or frozen, thawed
1 cup diced bell pepper
prepared quiche shell (see pages 5-15)
1/4 cup chopped fresh cilantro, optional
custard (pages 16-19)

Heat oven to 375°. Distribute corn and bell pepper evenly in quiche shell. Stir cilantro, if using, into custard. Cover corn-bell pepper mixture with custard and bake for 35 to 45 minutes, or until custard is set and top is lightly browned. Rest quiche for 5 minutes before cutting.

Makes one 9-inch quiche

VARIATIONS

- **SWEET CORN AND BACON QUICHE:** Substitute ½ lb. bacon, fried crisp and crumbled, for bell pepper. Omit cilantro.
- **SUCCOTASH QUICHE:** Reduce corn kernels to 1 cup and add 1 cup cooked baby lima beans. Substitute chopped fresh parsley for cilantro.
- **SOUTHWESTERN QUICHE**: Reduce corn kernels to 1 cup and add 1 cup cooked black beans and ¼ tsp. red pepper flakes.

QUICHE PRIMAVERA

Why not a fresh vegetable quiche? It's perfect vegetarian luncheon or brunch fare — add a crunchy green salad.

1 cup broccoli florets
1 cup thinly sliced carrots
1 cup diced red bell pepper
2-3 tbs. butter
3 large shallots, diced
prepared quiche shell (see pages 5-15)
1/4 cup chopped fresh chives
1/2 cup freshly grated Parmesan cheese
custard (see pages 16-19)

Heat oven to 375°. Steam broccoli, carrots and bell pepper or cook in boiling water until tender-crisp. Melt butter in a medium skillet and sauté shallots over medium heat for 2 to 3 minutes. Add broccoli, carrots and red bell pepper and toss to coat. Cool slightly. Arrange vegetable mixture in prepared quiche shell. Mix chives and cheese into custard and pour over vegetables. Bake for 35 to 45 minutes, or until custard is set and top is lightly browned. Rest quiche for 5 minutes before cutting.

Makes one 9-inch quiche

AVOCADO QUICHE

This rich quiche is perfect during the peak of avocado season. Use Haas avocados with bumpy black skin. Select avocados that are just ripe — overripe avocados will cause the quiche to be mushy.

3 avocados
1 tbs. lemon juice
prepared quiche shell (see pages 5-15)
1 cup diced red bell pepper
1/4 cup chopped fresh chives
custard (see pages 16-19)

Preheat oven to 375°. Halve, peel and pit avocados. Dice avocados and toss with lemon juice. Arrange in prepared quiche shell and sprinkle evenly with diced bell pepper. Mix chives into custard and pour over avocado. Bake for 35 to 45 minutes, until center is set and top is lightly browned. Rest quiche for 5 minutes before cutting.

Makes one 9-inch quiche

BROCCOLI CHEDDAR QUICHE

Broccoli is perfectly paired with cheddar for a richly flavored quiche.

½ lb. broccoli florets
prepared quiche shell (see pages 5-15)
1 cup grated sharp cheddar cheese
custard (see pages 16-19)

Heat oven to 375°. Break broccoli florets into small pieces. Steam broccoli or boil in water until tender-crisp. Drain well and sprinkle in prepared quiche shell. Sprinkle grated cheddar cheese evenly over broccoli and cover with custard. Bake for 35 to 45 minutes, or until custard is set and top is lightly browned. Rest quiche for 5 minutes before cutting.

Makes one 9-inch quiche

MUSHROOM QUICHE WITH ROASTED GARLIC

For a special occasion, choose shiitake, portobello
or other wild mushrooms.

1 bulb garlic
olive oil
2 tbs. chopped fresh rosemary,
   or 2 tsp. dried
custard (see pages 16-19)

½ lb. mushrooms
3 tbs. butter
prepared quiche shell (see
   pages 5-15)

Heat oven to 325°. Cut top from garlic bulb to expose cloves. Drizzle with olive oil and wrap in aluminum foil. Bake for about 1 hour. Remove from oven, and when cool enough to handle, squeeze garlic from bulb. Discard skins. Mix garlic pulp and rosemary with custard.

Increase oven heat to 375°. Clean mushrooms, remove stems and cut caps into quarters. Melt butter in a large skillet and sauté mushrooms over high heat until they have released all of their moisture,

about 10 minutes. Drain mushrooms well and distribute evenly in prepared quiche shell. Cover with custard and bake for 40 to 45 minutes, or until custard is set and top is lightly browned. Rest quiche for 5 minutes before cutting.

Makes one 9-inch quiche

VARIATIONS

- **MUSHROOM AND GREEN PEPPER QUICHE:** Omit rosemary and roasted garlic. Add 3 diced shallots to mushroom sauté. Add 2 medium green bell peppers, cut into small pieces, to mushroom sauté about halfway through cooking time.

- **MUSHROOM AND STRING BEAN QUICHE:** Omit rosemary. Steam or boil ½ lb. green beans, trimmed and cut into small pieces, until tender-crisp. Add to mushroom sauté about halfway through cooking time. Drain mushroom-green bean mixture well. Add ¼ cup chopped chives to custard.

SOUR CREAM MUSHROOM QUICHE

Use portobellos for a rich, meaty taste, shiitakes for an exotic taste or white button mushrooms for pure mushroom flavor. Or, try a combination.

3 tbs. butter
½ lb. mushrooms
2 tbs. dry sherry
prepared quiche shell (see pages 5-15)
Sour Cream Custard, page 18

Heat oven to 375°. In a large skillet, melt butter and sauté mushrooms over high heat until they have released all moisture, about 10 minutes. Cool slightly. Add sherry and continue cooking until all moisture has evaporated. Spread cooked mushrooms in prepared quiche shell and cover with sour cream custard. Bake for 40 to 45 minutes, or until custard is set and top is lightly browned. Rest quiche for 5 minutes before cutting.

Makes one 9-inch quiche

CARAMELIZED ONION QUICHE

The sweet, rich flavor of caramelized onions makes this quiche special. It's a good choice for an appetizer or party food.

4-5 medium yellow onions
1/4 cup butter
prepared quiche shell (see pages 5-15)
2 tsp. paprika
2 tbs. chopped fresh thyme, or 2 tsp. dried
custard (see pages 16-19)

Heat oven to 375°. Peel and slice onions. Melt butter in a large, heavy skillet and sauté onions over low heat until soft and brown, and all moisture has evaporated, about 35 to 40 minutes. Cool slightly. Spread onion slices evenly in prepared quiche shell. Add paprika and thyme to custard and beat until well blended. Pour custard over onions and bake for 35 to 45 minutes, or until custard is set and top is lightly browned. Rest quiche for 5 minutes before cutting.

Makes one 9-inch quiche

POTATO-ONION QUICHE

Fresh herbs are readily available in supermarkets, but you can always use dried herbs (about one-third of the amount of fresh herbs a recipe calls for) as a fall-back position.

2 lb. small red-skinned potatoes, cooked and diced
1 medium onion, diced
6 tbs. butter
prepared quiche shell (see pages 5-15)
2 tbs. chopped fresh rosemary, or 2 tsp. dried
custard (see pages 16-19)

Heat oven to 375°. In a medium, heavy skillet, melt butter and cook onion over medium heat until soft. Remove from heat, add potatoes and toss to coat with butter. Cool slightly. Arrange potato and onion in prepared quiche shell. Stir rosemary into custard and pour over potato and onion slices. Bake for 40 to 45 minutes, or until custard is set and top is lightly browned. Rest quiche for 5 minutes before cutting.

Makes one 9-inch quiche

VARIATION

- **POTATO, ONION AND BACON QUICHE:** Cook 6 slices bacon until crisp. Crumble and sprinkle over potato and onion slices before adding custard.

FRESH SPINACH QUICHE

If you don't have fresh spinach, use 1 package of frozen chopped spinach, thawed and squeezed dry.

1/4 cup butter
2 cloves garlic, minced
2 lb. fresh spinach, washed, stems removed
prepared quiche shell (see pages 5-15)
custard (see pages 16-19)

Heat oven to 375°. In a large skillet, melt butter over high heat. Add garlic and immediately add spinach, stirring until spinach is wilted. Remove from heat, cool slightly and spread spinach-garlic mixture in prepared quiche shell. Cover with custard and bake for 40 to 45 minutes, or until custard is set and top is lightly browned. Rest quiche for 5 minutes before cutting.

Makes one 9-inch quiche

VARIATIONS

- **FRESH SPINACH AND CHEESE QUICHE:** Sprinkle 1 cup grated Gruyère cheese over spinach in quiche shell before adding custard.

- **SOUR CREAM AND FRESH SPINACH QUICHE:** Use *Sour Cream Custard*, page 18.

EGGPLANT AND TOMATO QUICHE

*Enjoy classic Mediterranean flavors in this vegetable quiche.
The salting step removes bitterness from the eggplant
and is very important. To peel and seed a tomato, plunge into
boiling water for 15 to 30 seconds, depending on ripeness.
Remove peel with a small knife. Cut a small slice from the top of
the tomato and squeeze out seeds and juice.*

1 small eggplant
salt
flour
1 egg, beaten with 1 tbs. water
vegetable oil for frying
prepared quiche shell (see pages 5-15)
2 small tomatoes, peeled, seeded and sliced
¼ cup chopped fresh basil, or 1 heaping tbs. dried
custard (see pages 16-19)

Slice unpeeled eggplant and score slices with the tines of a fork. Sprinkle with salt and set aside in a colander for about 30 minutes. Wipe moisture from eggplant slices with paper towels.

Heat oven to 375°. Dredge eggplant slices in flour and then in egg mixture. Pour oil in a heavy skillet to about ½ inch. Bring to medium-high heat (about 380°) and fry eggplant slices on both sides until browned and crisp. Cool and drain on paper towels. Arrange a layer of eggplant slices in prepared quiche shell and cover with a layer of tomato slices. Sprinkle with basil. Repeat with remaining eggplant and tomato slices. Cover with custard and bake for 40 to 45 minutes, or until custard is set and top is lightly browned. Rest quiche for 5 minutes before cutting.

Makes one 9-inch quiche

CRAB QUICHE

The flavor of fresh crab that has never been frozen beats frozen or canned crab by far. But they can all be used in this recipe.

2 tbs. minced shallots
2 tbs. butter
1/2 lb. crabmeat, flaked
2 tbs. dry sherry
prepared quiche shell (see pages 5-15)
custard (see pages 16-19)
1/2 cup grated Gruyère or Swiss cheese

Heat oven to 375°. Sauté sallots in butter over medium heat until soft, 2 to 3 minutes. Add crabmeat and toss to coat with butter. Add sherry and cook until almost all liquid has evaporated. Cool slightly. Arrange crab-shallot mixture in prepared quiche shell. Pour custard over crab-shallot mixture and sprinkle cheese over all. Bake for 35 to 40 minutes or until custard is set and cheese is lightly browned. Rest quiche for 5 minutes before cutting.

Makes one 9-inch quiche

VARIATIONS

- **CRAB AND AVOCADO QUICHE:** Sprinkle 1 avocado, cut into ½-inch cubes, into prepared quiche shell with crabmeat before adding custard. Omit cheese.

- **CRAB AND PIMIENTO QUICHE:** Add 1 jar (4 oz.) chopped pimientos to crabmeat in quiche shell before adding custard. Omit cheese.

SHRIMP QUICHE

Shrimp makes a special quiche to serve to guests. Put some good wine into the recipe, and have the rest with a slice of the quiche after it's baked.

1/2 lb. medium-sized shrimp, peeled, deveined
2-3 tbs. butter
1/4 cup sliced green onions
1/2 cup dry white wine
1 tbs. Dijon mustard
prepared quiche shell (see pages 5-15)
1/4 cup chopped fresh flat-leaf parsley
custard (see pages 16-19)

Heat oven to 375°. In a medium saucepan, sauté shrimp in butter over medium-high heat until just cooked, about 2 minutes. Remove shrimp from pan. Reduce heat to medium. Add green onions to pan and sauté for 2 to 3 minutes. Add shrimp, wine and Dijon mustard

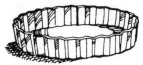

and continue to cook until liquid has evaporated. Cool slightly. Arrange shrimp mixture in prepared quiche shell. Add parsley to custard and mix well. Cover shrimp mixture with custard and bake for 35 to 40 minutes, or until custard is set and top is lightly browned. Rest quiche for 5 minutes before cutting.

Makes one 9-inch quiche

VARIATION

- **SPICY SHRIMP QUICHE:** Omit Dijon mustard, wine and parsley. Sauté 1 tbs. minced jalapeño pepper with the onions. Add shrimp to onion mixture and sprinkle with 2 tbs. lime juice. Continue to cook until liquid has evaporated. Arrange in prepared quiche shell with ½ cup chopped hearts of palm before adding custard.

LOBSTER THERMIDOR QUICHE

Reminiscent of the traditional dish, this quiche has the flavors of shallots, wine, mustard and tarragon. You can also use crab or shrimp in this recipe.

2 tbs. butter
$1/4$ cup chopped shallots
$1/2$ cup dry white wine
1 tbs. Dijon mustard
$1/4$ cup chopped fresh tarragon, or $1 1/2$ tsp. dried
$1/2$ lb. lobster meat, cut into small pieces
3 tbs. freshly grated Parmesan cheese
prepared quiche shell (see pages 5-15)
custard (see pages 16-19)

Heat oven to 375°. In a large skillet, melt butter and sauté shallots over medium heat until soft, about 2 to 3 minutes. Add wine and simmer until liquid is nearly evaporated. Remove from heat. Add mustard, tarragon, lobster meat and Parmesan, and toss until well combined. Cool slightly. Transfer mixture to prepared quiche shell and cover with custard. Bake for 35 to 40 minutes, or until custard is set and top is lightly browned. Rest quiche for 5 minutes before cutting.

Makes one 9-inch quiche

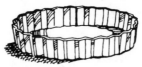

SMOKED SALMON, TOMATO AND DILL QUICHE

Smoked salmon makes an elegantly flavored quiche and an impressive addition to the buffet table.

3 tbs. chopped fresh dill, or 1 tbs. dried
custard (see pages 16-19)
¼ lb. thinly sliced smoked salmon
prepared quiche shell (see pages 5-15)
2 medium-sized plum tomatoes, peeled, seeded, diced

Heat oven to 375°. In a medium bowl, mix dill with custard until well distributed. Arrange pieces of salmon evenly in prepared quiche shell and sprinkle with tomato pieces. Cover with custard and bake for 40 to 45 minutes, or until custard is set and top is lightly browned. Rest quiche for 5 minutes before cutting.

Makes one 9-inch quiche

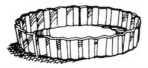

CHICKEN-PESTO QUICHE

Pesto makes everything taste wonderful. You can find it fresh, in containers in the refrigerator case at your supermarket near the fresh pasta, or frozen, or in tubes with the canned goods.

2 cups diced cooked chicken
1 cup diced roasted red pepper
prepared quiche shell (see pages 5-15)
$1/4$ cup pesto
custard (see pages 16-19)
$1/2$ cup freshly grated Parmesan cheese

Heat oven to 375°. Sprinkle chicken and roasted red pepper evenly in prepared quiche shell. Stir pesto into custard. Cover chicken-red pepper mixture with custard and sprinkle with Parmesan cheese. Bake for 35 to 45 minutes, or until custard is set and top is lightly browned. Rest quiche for 5 minutes before cutting.

Makes one 9-inch quiche

CHICKEN QUICHE SOUTHWESTERN-STYLE

A chile pepper, fresh cilantro and queso fresco are added to chicken to form a spicy version of a chicken quiche. If you can't find queso fresco (Mexican-style fresh white cheese), substitute feta. Poblano chiles are sometimes mistakenly called pasillas in the produce section of your store.

2 tbs. butter
1 small onion, chopped
1 poblano chile, stemmed, seeded, chopped
2 cups diced cooked chicken
prepared quiche shell (see pages 5-15)
1/2 cup crumbled queso fresco or feta cheese
1/4 cup chopped fresh cilantro
custard (see pages 16-19)

Heat oven to 375°. Melt butter in a large skillet. Add onion and poblano chile and sauté over medium heat until vegetables are soft, 3 to 5 minutes. Add chicken and stir to mix. Cool slightly. Transfer mixture to prepared quiche shell and spread evenly. Add cheese and cilantro to custard. Cover chicken mixture with custard and bake for 35 to 45 minutes, or until custard is set and top is lightly browned. Rest quiche for 5 minutes before cutting.

Makes one 9-inch quiche

CHICKEN AND MUSHROOM QUICHE

Chicken owes some of its popularity to its ability to blend well with almost any flavor. The addition of goat cheese, fresh thyme and sun-dried tomatoes adds distinctive tastes to this quiche. If you use dry-packed sun-dried tomatoes for this recipe, rehydrate them first in boiling water to cover for about 5 minutes, and then drain them well before cutting them into slivers.

2 tbs. butter
½ lb. mushrooms, finely sliced
1 cup diced cooked chicken
½ cup slivered oil-packed sun-dried tomatoes
prepared quiche shell (see pages 5-15)
½ cup crumbled goat cheese
¼ cup chopped fresh thyme
custard (see pages 16-19)

Heat oven to 375°. In a large skillet, melt butter over medium-high heat. Sauté mushrooms until they have released all of their moisture, about 10 minutes. Stir in chicken and sun-dried tomatoes and remove from heat. Cool slightly. Pour chicken mixture into prepared quiche shell. Add goat cheese and thyme to custard and stir well. Cover chicken mixture with custard and bake for 35 to 45 minutes, until custard is set and top is lightly browned. Rest quiche for 5 minutes before cutting.

Makes one 9-inch quiche

QUICHE WITH CHICKEN, PROSCIUTTO AND MOZZARELLA

Fresh mozzarella is packaged in whey or water. It is softer and has a more delicate flavor than regular mozzarella, and you can use it as a spread. It melts nicely in this quiche.

2 cups diced cooked chicken
½ cup chopped prosciutto
½ cup diced well-drained fresh mozzarella cheese
¼ cup chopped fresh basil, or 1 heaping tbs. dried
prepared quiche shell (see pages 5-15)
custard (see pages 16-19)

Heat oven to 375°. Distribute chicken, prosciutto and mozzarella evenly in prepared quiche shell. Add chopped basil to custard and mix well. Pour custard over chicken mixture. Bake for 35 to 40 minutes, until custard is set and top is lightly browned. Rest quiche for 5 minutes before cutting.

Makes one 9-inch quiche

SMOKED TURKEY QUICHE

*The slightly bitter flavor of the arugula is the perfect
counterpoint to the creamy Gorgonzola and the
distinctive flavor of the smoked turkey.*

2 cups diced smoked turkey, or
⅔ lb. sliced smoked turkey, cut into strips
prepared quiche shell (see pages 5-15)
½ cup crumbled Gorgonzola cheese
¼ cup chopped arugula
custard (see pages 16-19)

Heat oven to 375°. Distribute turkey evenly in prepared quiche shell. Stir Gorgonzola and arugula into custard. Pour custard over turkey and bake for 35 to 45 minutes, until custard is set and top is lightly browned. Rest quiche for 5 minutes before cutting.

Makes one 9-inch quiche

CORNED BEEF AND POTATO QUICHE

The ingredients found in one of your favorite breakfast dishes, corned beef hash, produce the perfect fare for brunch.

1/2 cup diced onion
2 tbs. butter
1 cup diced cooked corned beef
1 cup diced cooked red-skinned potatoes with skins
1 tsp. caraway seeds
prepared quiche shell (see pages 5-15)
1 tbs. Dijon mustard
custard (see pages 16-19)
1 cup grated Gruyère cheese

Heat oven to 375°. In a large skillet, sauté onion in butter over medium heat for 3 to 4 minutes, until soft. Remove from heat and cool slightly. Add corned beef, potatoes and caraway seeds and toss to coat. Distribute hash mixture evenly in prepared quiche shell. Add Dijon mustard to custard and mix well. Cover hash with custard and sprinkle with cheese. Bake for 35 to 45 minutes, until custard is set and top is lightly browned. Rest quiche for 5 minutes before cutting.

Makes one 9-inch quiche

ITALIAN SAUSAGE QUICHE

*Italian sausages seem to make any dish irresistible, and adding
sun-dried tomatoes and smoked Gouda only makes it better.*

1/2 lb. Italian sausages, mild or hot
prepared quiche shell (see pages 5-15)
1/2 cup chopped oil-packed sun-dried tomatoes
1/2 cup grated smoked Gouda cheese
custard (see pages 16-19)

Heat oven to 375°. Cook sausages in casings in a skillet over
medium heat until cooked through. When cool enough to handle,
remove casings and cut into 1/2-inch rounds. Distribute sausage slices
evenly in prepared quiche shell and sprinkle with sun-dried tomatoes
and grated cheese. Cover with custard and bake for 35 to 45 minutes,
until custard is set and top is lightly browned. Rest quiche for 5
minutes before cutting.

Makes one 9-inch quiche

INDEX